Footsteps to Follow™
Daniel

The *Footsteps to Follow*™ series of books is designed to present the principals and characters of the bible to young readers. In doing this, narration is added and adaptation of the word is made so that the translation is age appropriate.

Daniel is dedicated to all young boys who share his name. This book is offered so that they may better understand his life and grow up to be faithful servants of God.

Currently Available: Available in 1998:

Daniel   *Joseph*

David   *Birth of Jesus*

Library of Congress Catalog Card Number: 97-76769
ISBN: 0-9657091-2-4

DANIEL

As told by **Mandy Peterson**
Illustrated by **Sarah Hill Green**

DANIEL OF JERUSALEM

This is a story about a young boy, Daniel, who lived in the city of Jerusalem. He was the son of a royal official and attended school in the palace. Daniel's teacher, Jeremiah, made learning fun. Jeremiah was not only a good teacher, he was also a messenger of God to the people of Jerusalem.

One day while the boys were out playing, they heard a familiar voice coming from the town square. They ran over and were surprised to see their teacher.

"Your greed and love of money is not pleasing God," Jeremiah told the crowd. "God wants us to love him and one another. If you do not change your ways, God will stop protecting you. A huge army is coming to invade the city," Jeremiah proclaimed. "Without God's protection, we will lose everything - our freedom, families, homes, and possessions."

Daniel and his friends looked around at the people who had come to hear Jeremiah speak. They were all laughing and making fun of him.

"Why are all these people laughing?" Daniel asked. "Don't they know Jeremiah tells the truth. What he says is really scary. What do you guys think?"

"I think the people should listen," replied one of Daniel's friends. "What he says is right, all anyone cares about is making money."

Daniel said, "No one seems to remember God's love. They aren't following His commandments. I'm going to ask my father about Jeremiah's warnings."

DANIEL SPEAKS TO HIS FATHER

Daniel left his friends and hurried home to tell his dad what Jeremiah had said. His father was surprised to see Daniel running. "Daniel, my son, what's the matter? You are all out of breath."

"Father," Daniel said, "Jeremiah is telling everyone that God is REALLY upset with Jerusalem. Very few people are obeying His ten commandments because they are sooo busy making money. He says some guy named Neba, uh, Nebacheeser, no, Nebasneezer, no."

Daniel's father laughed and hugged him tight. "It's Nebuchadnezzar."

"Okay! Okay! Anyway, this bad king and his huge army are coming to attack Jerusalem! Will they really attack us?" asked Daniel.

"Well, possibly. And if they do, our army will fight back. But, no matter what happens, remember God loves us," his father replied.

"Why doesn't God just wipe out this Nebuchadnezzar guy? He could wipe the whole army out with one big breath…WHOOSH!"

Daniel's father said, "Remember Jeremiah's warning. If the people don't listen, God may not protect us from our enemies. It's like when you disobey, I may punish you even though I love you. In the same way, God loves us and wants us to follow His rules. When we forget, though, we must face the consequences."

"I guess God is like the whole world's father," Daniel said. "I'm going to pray that the people listen."

THE FALL OF JERUSALEM

Jeremiah had spoken the truth, but the people did not listen. Soon, the Babylonian army surrounded Jerusalem. They had the largest, strongest, most powerful army in the world. The people of Jerusalem were afraid; they were no match for these warriors.

For many months the army surrounded the city, cutting off all food and supplies. Slowly, the people of Jerusalem ran out of food. Rather than starve to death, they surrendered.

Daniel watched as the Babylonian army entered the city gates. He ran to his father crying, "What is going to happen now? I am afraid!"

"You must be strong, Daniel, put your faith in God," his father assured him.

Meanwhile, King Nebuchadnezzar was shouting orders to his men. "Take the treasure from the temple! Remove all the gold and silver from the city! Gather up the skilled workers and educated people! They will be my servants! Make them carry the treasure back to Babylon! Destroy the temple and burn the city! Leave the sick and old behind!"

Later that day, Daniel, his father, and thousands of captives began the five-hundred-mile walk to Babylon. Among the captives, Daniel found his friends and walked with them. The young boys struggled to carry the heavy bags of treasure. The guards shouted at them to go faster and seldom let them rest. They feared they would not survive the journey.

JOURNEY TO BABYLON

Daniel and his friends looked back one last time and saw Jerusalem in flames. Just as Jeremiah said, without God's protection, they had lost everything. Days became weeks, and weeks turned into months. As they traveled, they wondered what life would be like in Babylon.

When they finally reached Babylon, the boys had to march across a bridge to enter. Below them, water rushed in the moat that ran alongside a great wall surrounding the city. Walking through the gates, they saw huge buildings, soldiers marching, and strange statues everywhere.

As they were led through the city, the boys saw paved streets and winding canals. They were surprised at all the colorful decorations. Each street had buildings with different designs and colors.

"Daniel, Daniel, look over there!" shouted one of the boys. "That building is covered with pictures of blue horses with wings on yellow tiles!"

"Look at that street! It's orange with white statues on it!" replied Daniel.

Daniel turned to his father and said, "The strange statues in the streets give me a weird feeling. I feel like they're watching me. What are they for?"

"Those are the things the Babylonians worship. They don't realize they only need to worship God," Daniel's father said.

Inside his palace, Nebuchadnezzar ordered his guards, "Go among the Jews and bring the smartest young boys to work for me! Then tell my counselors and wise men to come here! I'm gone for a few months and everyone forgets their job! What is a king to do?"

LIFE IN BABYLON

Daniel and his three friends were chosen to work for the king. The time had come for Daniel to leave his father. Sadness overwhelmed him as he realized he might never see his father again. Daniel gave him a big hug.

Daniel's father held him close and said, "I am your earthly father, and I'll love you forever. Always remember, your heavenly Father will go with you where I can't."

Daniel fought back tears as he and his friends were led away by the guards into the strange palace.

"Welcome!" said one of the king's wise men. For the first time in many months, the boys heard their own language spoken by a Babylonian.

"The king has chosen you to learn about our customs and laws," the wise man explained to the group of boys. "He wants you to forget your Jewish way of life and become Babylonians."

"Daniel," his friend whispered, "We can't just forget about God."

"You're right. As children of God, we must pray to Him and follow His laws," replied Daniel quietly.

"The first thing I will do is give you new Babylonian names," the wise man shouted. "No more silly Jewish names." Daniel was named Belteshazzar. His three friends were called Shadrach, Meshach and Abednego.

"Oh, no," the boys grumbled. "We can't pronounce any of these."

"Don't worry," Daniel said. "We will always have our real names, even if we are the only ones who remember them."

DANIEL'S FIRST TEST

The king wanted the new students to be healthy and happy. He sent food from the royal kitchen for them to eat. When the boys entered the dining hall, they saw tables piled high with meats, breads, cheeses, vegetables, and wine.

Daniel looked at his friends and said, "We can't eat this meat. God told Moses we shouldn't eat pigs, rabbits, camels, lizards and crabs. These tables are filled with all of those. I will go to the chief official and tell him we would like to have just vegetables, bread, and water."

"Vegetables, bread, and water?" the surprised official asked. "I have never heard of young boys wanting to eat only vegetables!"

"My friends and I cannot eat these meats," Daniel explained.

"The king ordered this food for you," the official said. "If you don't eat, the king will be mad. You really don't want to see what happens when he gets angry!"

Daniel did not give up. "Please, sir, let us eat this way for ten days and you will see that we do not need to eat meat to be strong and healthy," he said.

The chief official reluctantly agreed and let them eat only bread and vegetables like peas and beans. After ten days the official saw that they looked healthier than the other boys who had eaten the meats. From that day on, Daniel and his friends were allowed to eat as they had asked. For their faithfulness, God blessed the boys. He gave them gifts of great knowledge and understanding.

The boys learned to speak, read and write the language of Babylon. They studied history, science, astrology, and local customs. After living in the palace for three years, the boys were called before King Nebuchadnezzar.

"My goodness, look at these four healthy lads," said the king. "They seem to be doing very well." He turned to the boys and said, "I will test each of you to see how much you have learned."

They were able to answer all the king's questions. The king was amazed! "Why these boys are the smartest I have ever seen! They are ten times smarter than the others! I want these four to be my advisors."

So, Daniel, Shadrach, Meshach, and Abednego began their work as the king's advisors.

NEBUCHADNEZZAR'S DREAM

The boys soon discovered being advisors would not be an easy job. Late one night the king was awakened by a terrible nightmare. He called for his advisors. Within minutes the king's room was filled with people.

"I want to know the meaning of my dream!" the king demanded.

"Tell us your dream and we'll tell you its meaning," his advisors replied.

"I can't remember it all! You are my wise men, magicians, and sorcerers! You should know! You must explain it to me! If you tell me what it means, I will give you gifts and treasure. If you fail, heads will roll!" the king shouted.

"But, your majesty, you are the only one who has seen your dream. This is too hard," the advisors whined. "Only a god could see someone else's dream."

The king exploded with anger, "You dare tell your great king that it is impossible?! You shall be put to death!"

Daniel had been standing at the back of the room. "Oh great king, give me some time and I may be able to help," he said.

"I will give you until morning, but if you don't tell me about my dream, heads will roll!" the king roared.

That night, Daniel and his friends prayed together for God to show them the dream. As Daniel slept, he saw the king's dream and understood its meaning.

The next morning Daniel reported to King Nebuchadnezzar, "O king, I know all about your dream."

"I knew you were my best magician!" the excited king answered.

"No," Daniel replied. "My power is not through magic, nor am I wiser than anyone else. God revealed your dream to me so that I could explain it to you. In your dream, you saw a huge statue with a gold head and a body made of other metals. Suddenly, a rock fell from the sky and smashed the statue's foot. The statue fell - CRASH! It broke apart and was blown away by the wind. Then the rock grew bigger and bigger until it was the size of a mountain."

"Yes, yes, that's my dream!" the king answered, "but what does it mean?"

"Your dream reveals all the great kingdoms of the world. The statue's gold head represents your kingdom, Babylon. It will be the richest. After Babylon, there will be a kingdom called Medo-Persia which won't be as great as yours. It is shown by the silver chest and arms. The bronze stomach and thighs represent Greece, which will be even weaker. The iron legs and clay feet stand for the kingdom of Rome."

"All those kingdoms are nothing next to the rock that becomes a mountain. The mountain is the most powerful kingdom, the kingdom of God. God wants you to see that His kingdom will rule even after all the others are gone."

Nebuchadnezzar fell to his knees in front of Daniel. "Your God says my kingdom will be the greatest? Your God is wise and so are you. I want you to be in charge of all my advisors."

Daniel accepted and became the king's most trusted advisor.

INTO THE FIRE

As chief advisor, Daniel traveled all over the kingdom while his friends stayed busy working in the palace. Nebuchadnezzar was busy too, busy thinking about his dream. His mind was filled with thoughts of a huge gold statue of himself. It would be 90 feet high and 90 feet wide so it could be seen from any place in the city. He called for his builders and ordered them to build it immediately!

When the statue was finished, Nebuchadnezzar ordered everyone to gather around it.

"My people!" the king shouted. "I am the greatest king of all time and you shall worship me like a god. Today we have a new law. Every time you hear music, you must fall to your knees and bow to this statue. Those who do not obey will be thrown into the fiery furnace!"

The people gasped as they looked at the huge oven the builders used to bake bricks. Smoke poured from the opening as the fire roared in the furnace.

Shadrach, Meshach, and Abednego were amazed at what the king had said. Abednego turned to his friends. "We cannot worship this statue! We must remain faithful to God and His laws!" The other two agreed.

The next day when the people heard music, they fell to their knees and worshipped the giant statue of the king. Shadrach, Meshach and Abednego did not kneel. A guard saw the three standing and ordered them to kneel. When they refused, they were taken before the king.

Nebuchadnezzar was furious! "Why did you break the law?" he yelled.

"We can only worship the one true God," Shadrach explained.

"I say you must worship me! I'll give you one more chance. Fall to your knees and I will let you live. If you do not, you will be thrown into the furnace. What god will save you from that awful heat, HUH?" the king said angrily.

Shadrach, Meshach and Abednego shook their heads and said, "We do not need to explain this to you. Our faith is in God. He has the power to save us, but even if we are to die, we will only worship Him."

"You are willing to die for this God?" the king asked.

"Yes, we would rather suffer than turn against God," replied Shadrach.

"OK! I'll show you what hot means!" The king shouted to his guards, "I want the fire seven times hotter!"

"But king," the guard said, "we can't even get to the fire when it's that hot."

The king's face became red. "I want the fire HOTTER!! These three say I am not as important as some invisible God! I will show them who is powerful!!"

Shadrach, Meshach and Abednego were tied together and led to the furnace.

"Throw them in!!" the king ordered.

The fire was so hot that the heat killed the guards as they pushed Shadrach, Meshach and Abednego into the fiery furnace. As the fire blazed, Nebuchadnezzar looked into the giant furnace. "Wait!" the king said jumping to his feet. "Didn't we only throw three men in the fire? Why do I see four?"

"Yes, there were only three men," his advisors agreed.

THE ANGEL'S MESSAGE

The king looked at the fire again and it was clear that four men were walking around inside the furnace. The king walked closer to the furnace and shouted, "Shadrach! Meshach! Abednego! Come out of the furnace!"

The three men walked out of the fire. The advisors and guards were amazed. They touched them, but nothing was burnt. They didn't even smell like smoke.

Then suddenly, the fourth figure flew out of the fire and approached the king saying, "I am the Archangel Michael, protector of all who serve the True Living God. God saved these three because they were faithful! God has given you the power to rule the people, but YOU are not a god! You must believe in God and rule by His commandments."

Nebuchadnezzar fell to the ground saying, "I was wrong. I will serve God."

Then the clouds opened and the angel flew up into heaven.

The king turned to the crowd. "Shadrach, Meshach and Abednego told me that they would not bow down to my statue. They had faith and their God protected them. We cannot deny the power of the God of these three men. From now on, the people of Babylon will be allowed to worship this God in peace."

Although Nebuchadnezzar praised God, he did not follow God's commandments. He spoke about God, but he lived according to his own laws.

NEBUCHADNEZZAR'S NEXT DREAM

One night the king had another scary nightmare. Since he didn't understand it, he called his chief advisor, Daniel, to interpret the dream. As Daniel entered, the king said, "I have had another dream which is so awful I cannot sleep. God allowed you to see my last dream, so I am sure you can explain this one."

"Tell me your dream and I will listen for God's message," Daniel replied.

"First, there is this giant tree. From the top you can see all the earth. Birds live in its branches, animals and people live in its shade. The fruit of the tree feeds all the men and animals on earth. It is a very nice dream until suddenly, the sky gets dark! An angel holding a sword comes down from heaven. With one mighty blow -WHACK - he chops down the tree! Only the stump of the tree is left."

"Now comes the scary part! This strange, wild creature comes out of the forest and sits next to the stump. It looks half human and half beast. It eats the bugs crawling from the stump. I have never seen anything like it before! Why would I have such a horrible dream?"

The meaning of the dream worried Daniel. He was afraid to tell the king, but knew he must. "The giant tree represents you. God is warning you to follow His commandments, not just talk about them," said Daniel.

"I have already praised God to the people. What more does He want?" the king asked.

"Your words don't mean anything if you don't have God in your heart and mind. If you don't listen and obey Him, He will cut you down like the tree and you will become the creature in your dream," Daniel explained.

Nebuchadnezzar laughed. "Eat bugs and live like an animal? Lose my kingdom? I don't think so!"

"I know it is hard to believe. But the tree stump shows God's promise for a second chance. Your kingdom will be restored and the tree will grow again when you decide to follow God's commandments. You should listen to what God is telling you," said Daniel.

For a while the king followed Daniel's advice. However, as time passed, Nebuchadnezzar forgot God's commandments. One day the king said to himself, "I rule the richest kingdom in the world. I am truly as mighty as a god!"

Suddenly, the sky above grew dark! The angel of his dream appeared and said, "Your dream is about to come true."

Filled with fear, the king ran from the palace and hid in the forest. There he lived like an animal for seven years. One day while Nebuchadnezzar was getting a drink from a pond, he saw his reflection. Looking back at him was the creature of his dream. He knew that Daniel was right. He fell to his knees and cried out to God, "Oh Lord, You are the one true God. I am nothing. Please forgive me."

Looking up, he saw Daniel coming toward him. Nebuchadnezzar knew God had forgiven him. The king returned to Babylon and ruled by God's commandments until his death.

THE WRITING ON THE WALL

Now, the new king of Babylon, Belshazzar, did not believe in God. He was selfish and did not love anyone but himself. One night he had a grand party with thousands of guests.

"Look at these tiny cups," Belshazzar said. "I'm far too important for these things. Bring me the goblets Nebuchadnezzar took from that temple in Jerusalem."

The servants returned shortly with the gold goblets. They filled them with wine for the king and his most honored guests. "Mmm," he said, "I can't believe I have never used these before."

Just then, a giant hand appeared behind the king. Screaming echoed through the room. "O King!" a guard said in a trembling voice, "look behind you! A hand is writing on the wall! No arm! No body! Nothing but a hand!" The king turned to look and fainted at the sight of the hand.

"EEKKK!" the guests screamed as the hand disappeared.

The room was silent as the king was revived. "Get my advisors! I want to know what that says!"

The king's advisors tried to read the message, but none of them could. The guests were frightened and began to leave. Then the queen turned to Belshazzar and said, "I remember Nebuchadnezzar had an advisor who could explain dreams. Maybe he can help."

The king ordered his men to bring Daniel to the palace. When Daniel arrived, Belshazzar told him, "If you can tell me the meaning of the words, I will give you a beautiful robe and a gold chain."

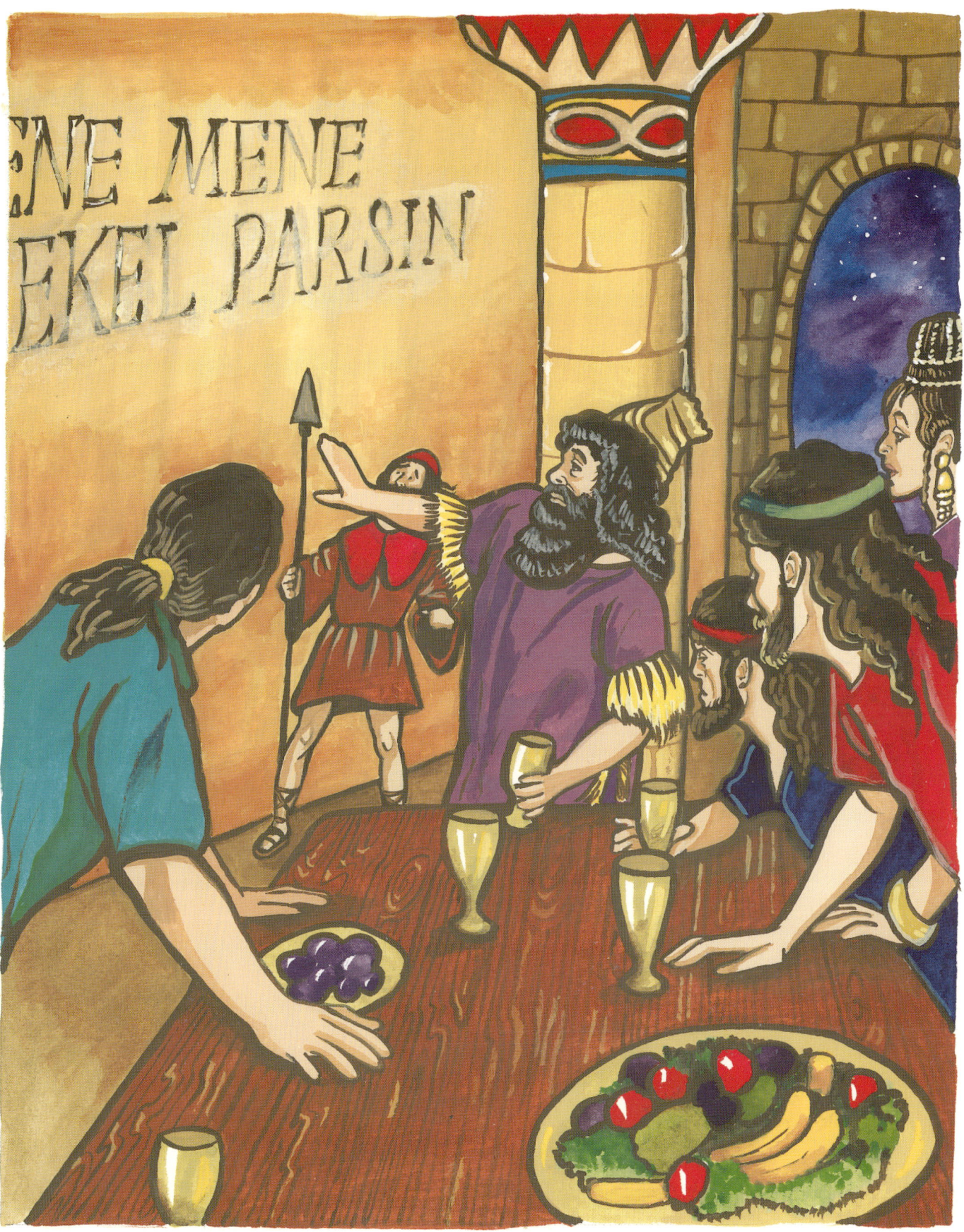

"I don't need any gifts," Daniel said to the king. "I will tell you what the words mean. Like you, Nebuchadnezzar thought he was a god and should be worshipped. Do you remember when he lived like an animal? Only after he believed in God was his kingdom restored."

"Of course, I remember when he lived in the forest! He thought he was an animal!" the king laughed. "Now, tell me what the words on the wall mean!"

Daniel shook his head. "God is upset with you because you drank from his holy cup. He is sending you a message."

Belshazzar rolled his eyes and shouted, "OK! OK! What IS the message?"

"There are four words on the wall," Daniel said. "The first two, *MENE MENE*, mean your days are finished as king. The next word, *TEKEL*, means you are not worthy to be king. The last, *PARSIN*, means your kingdom will be divided."

Belshazzar said, "I don't believe you, but you may have the robe and chains as promised."

"I do not care about the gifts," Daniel told the king. "I only wish you would believe in God."

That very night, Belshazzar died. The kingdom of Babylon ended, and the Medo-Persian kingdom began with Darius the Mede as king.

IN THE LION'S DEN

The new king, Darius, trusted Daniel and made him his chief advisor. The two men became close friends. The other advisors became jealous of Daniel's position and his friendship with the king.

"He's not even royalty," one of the advisors mumbled.

"Yeah, he's one of those boys from Jerusalem that old Nebuchadnezzar took as a slave," another replied. "We need to find a way to get rid of that guy."

The men tried to catch Daniel doing something wrong, but he always did what was right. They came up with a plan to make Daniel choose between serving God or the king.

"O Great King," the men praised Darius. "You are so mighty and wonderful! You should make everyone bow down and worship you!"

"Well, well," the king said, "I am pretty wonderful! What should I do?"

"You could make a law that forbids the worship of anyone but you for thirty days. Maybe even put it in writing so no one can change it," one man suggested.

"If anyone breaks the law, they will be thrown into a den of lions," said another.

"That's great! Write it up and post it around the city," the king exclaimed.

"Oh, Yes! Now we just have to wait and watch Daniel," one of the advisors whispered to another. "He will pray to his God and then we'll have him."

A few days later they saw Daniel praying to God and ran to tell the king.

"O King, O King," his advisors cried, "we saw Daniel praying to his God. He is breaking the law!"

Darius was upset. He liked Daniel very much and didn't want to punish him. "Well, we will just have to change that law," he said.

"Even you can't change a written law after it's been posted," the advisors said as they slyly grinned at each other.

The king then realized his advisors only wanted to get Daniel in trouble. He tried to find a way to save his friend from the lions. But there was nothing he could do. He called for Daniel.

"Daniel, my friend," the king said sadly. "You have been seen worshipping someone other than me. I have tried to save you, but I cannot change a written law. I was wrong to make that dumb law and ask you to worship me. Please forgive me, but I have to put you in the lion's den."

"My friend and king, I forgive you. I know God will be with me," Daniel replied.

As the guards threw Daniel into the lion's den, King Darius cried out, "May your God protect you." Sadly, the king went back to his palace.

The sly advisors tried to make the king happy. "Would you like some food? Maybe your musicians can play for you."

"I don't want anything!" Darius snapped. That night the king tossed and turned. He knew his pride had cost Daniel his life. He felt very ashamed.

The next morning the king awoke and ran to the lion's den. He knew in his heart that his friend was dead, but he shouted anyway. "Daniel! Daniel! Please tell me that your God saved you!"

To his surprise, Darius heard a voice come from the den, "Yes, my king, I am safe. God sent an angel to close the lions' mouths."

The king ordered his guards to remove Daniel from the den. When he came out, Darius gave him a hug. King Darius saw the men who had accused Daniel trying to sneak away. "I want them thrown into the den!" he told his guards.

Daniel and the king walked away as the hungry lions enjoyed their breakfast feast. From that day on, King Darius declared that everyone should worship Daniel's God.

DANIEL'S LIFE

After Daniel was saved, the people could once again worship God in peace. The angel of God frequently visited Daniel and showed him many visions.

The angel told Daniel, "Someday, Jesus will come, but most people will not believe he is God's son. All those who believe and follow Him will rise up to heaven and live forever. The wicked will be left behind."

Daniel faithfully served the remainder of his life as an advisor to Darius and the next king, Cyrus. As he grew older, Daniel never forgot Jeremiah telling the people they would be captives in Babylon for seventy years. After that time had passed, he knew the people should return home to Jerusalem.

Daniel went to King Cyrus and asked permission. The King agreed and even said he could go with them.

"Although I am very glad my people will be allowed to return," Daniel explained, "I will follow God's will and stay here."

Thus, Daniel did as God asked until the day he died.

You can follow Daniel's footsteps in the following ways:
- *Learn and follow God's commandments;*
- *Pray that you may follow God's will;*
- *Be faithful to God and He will bless you;*
- *Know that God is with you wherever you are;*
- *Love God, He is your heavenly father.*